STUDIES IN MODERN EUROPEAN LITERATURE AND THOUGHT

General Editor:
E R I C H   H E L L E R
Professor of German
in the University College of Swansea

LÉON BLOY

LÉON BLOY

BY

RAYNER HEPPENSTALL

NEW HAVEN
YALE UNIVERSITY PRESS
1954

CONTENTS

Part One

In the late autumn of 1935, I embarked upon a religious conversion which eventually proved abortive. I had lost my faith in political revolution. My situation was that of the young provincial starving as manfully as he could in a London garret. This was in Kentish Town, and I shared it with George Orwell, ten years my senior. I had recently become estranged from Mr J. Middleton Murry, with whom I had been staying in Norfolk as a kind of secretary, but I enjoyed the friendship of Herbert Read and the encouragement of Eric Gill. My conversion began under the very best auspices. In no time at all I was at Campion Hall, receiving instruction from Father D'Arcy.

In Oxford I read the letters of G. M. Hopkins and copied out what he says about the Greek gods as poetical machinery, as well as his beautiful distinction between the meanings of the word 'mystery' to non-Catholics (for whom it is 'an interesting uncertainty') and to Catholics (for whom it is 'an incomprehensible certainty'). I read Traherne and St John of the Cross. I made some progress with a long poem. I encountered the intellectual difficulties which more successful converts somehow surmount. It was, I discovered, one thing to perceive what a blessing it is to be a Catholic, to wake in the night and hug oneself with pleasure at the thought that now everything will be different because one is going to be a Catholic and that presently one will wake in the night rejoicing that one is a Catholic already. It was quite another matter to believe, in any literal sense, what the church requires one to profess to believe, and, wriggle as I might, I did not see how I could bring myself to profess to believe certain things unless I had first contrived to make myself believe that I did. However, doubts of this kind are an accepted part of the routine.

Leaving Campion Hall and returning to London, I continued to receive instruction from an older Jesuit at Farm Street and to read approved books.

I was introduced to a number of young Catholics, of whom two who remain my friends were Bernard and Barbara Wall. After a quarrel of some violence, I parted company with George

7

Orwell and went to live in Mortimer Market, off Tottenham Court Road, over a scissors grinder. Here, I ate far too little. Orwell had always had food, which he cooked with great skill.

The Walls and their friends were torn between the claims of action and those of contemplation. One of the young men was proposing to enter a Trappist monastery. Another, a man of the purest genius of whom I no longer hear anything, Bernard Kelly, was a bank clerk who lived philoprogenitively in the suburbs. Their political hopes were pinned on the Jocistes ('*Jeunesse Ouvrière Chrétienne*'), and after mass on Sunday morning they sold *The Catholic Worker* outside churches. They had an extensive slang of their own, and this, for instance, they called 'doing masses'. Bernard Wall edited a crusading quarterly called *Colosseum*. He and his wife, a grand-daughter of Alice Meynell, had travelled much abroad, and *Colosseum* was cosmopolitan in outlook.

Among the writers, hitherto unknown to me, of whom it spoke was Léon Bloy. There were translated extracts from his *Exégèse des Lieux Communs*, and there was an article on him by Jacques Maritain, whose name I well knew, who was, it appeared, a convert and godson of Bloy's and who stated that his godfather had written the greatest French prose since Bossuet. From Bernard Wall, I borrowed copies of *Le Désespéré*, the earlier and longer of Bloy's two novels, and *Le Pèlerin de l'Absolu*, the sixth volume of his published journals.

An idea strongly represented in *Colosseum* was that communism is merely the ultimate form of nineteenth-century capitalism and that true revolution lies apart from either. To me, this idea was novel and pleasing. Despite Eric Gill, I had supposed Catholicism essentially non-revolutionary. I had even, with Karl Marx, regarded it as the opium of the people. And I was at heart a revolutionary. It was therefore reassuring to find grounds for supposing that I could remain a revolutionary even under conversion. Father D'Arcy might be an old Tory, but not these young believers who made fun of him as a diner-out with countesses. And not, I found, Léon Bloy, to whom the *bourgeoisie* was as hateful as ever I had been led to suppose.

It was also at this time that I first read *The Brothers Karamazov*.

8

In Bloy there was the same violence, the same cultivation of the extremes of joy and despair, as in Dostoevski. Indeed, if anything, Bloy was the more violent of the two—in his language, at least. Here was no milk-and-water pietism, but a religion passionate and heroic, to which the '*bondieuserie sulpicienne*' of '*les bien-pensants*' was as repugnant as anything I might see or imagine at Oxford, a faith which permitted the believer to regard even the general run of priests as malignant imbeciles and for which Maritain yet vouched that it in no way militated against the requirements of true charity.

In Bloy's exegesis of the commonplace, the *bourgeois* is the man who has bowed down and received the mark of the Beast and the smoke of whose torments shall rise up from generation to generation, whence his own comfortable saying that there is no smoke without fire. The other commonplaces upon which *Colosseum* showed Bloy's mind playing ironically and vindictively were those which proclaim that business is business, that health comes first and that appetite comes with eating—a good answer, as Bloy says, to a man dying of hunger. Altogether, Bloy isolated and examined three hundred and ten examples of the proverbial wisdom of the French middle classes, a majority of which have their frighteningly exact counterparts in English.

Bloy's diaries personify him by their titles. He is in turn the ungrateful beggar (*Le Mendiant Ingrat*), the provincial caged lion (*Quatre Ans de Captivité à Cochons-sur-Marne*), the man who cannot be sold (*L'Invendable*), the old man of the mountains (*Le Vieux de la Montagne*, but the mountain in question is the '*butte* de Montmartre'), the pilgrim of the absolute (*Le Pèlerin de l'Absolu*), one standing before the apocalyptical threshold (*Au Seuil de l'Apocalypse*) and venturing finally through the gateway of the humble (*La Porte des Humbles*). From *Le Pèlerin de l'Absolu*, two entries which lodged in my mind concerned a priest's carelessness at mass and a journalist's view of the sacramental function of public houses. A consecrated host fell to the floor and was allowed to remain there—'the body of Christ', exclaims Bloy, 'lying on the ground'—disregarded. This frightened me. That the wafer becomes substantially Christ's body Catholics believe, but not, one had thought, quite so literally. A writer whose name Bloy does

9

not record—'I shall have forgotten it in a quarter of an hour'—
had published in *Paris-Journal* an article in which he says that
drink has a ritual value and that the drinker is *'une sorte de
communiant'*:

> In our time, as the old religions lose one by one their sanct-
> uaries and their congregations, a public house is one of the
> places in which new human bonds are elaborated, new relig-
> ious stirrings, new participations in the Divine. I shall admit,
> if pressed, that humanity, avid of communion, could have
> chosen better places... But our time rejects the deliberate crea-
> tion of great human festivals... Let us therefore be content
> with the spontaneous and sincere if rather second-rate crea-
> tions offered us, and let us honour, with a devotion largely
> made up of hope, our public houses, those interim churches.

Bloy's reaction is one of pure contempt. This also worried me
a little. Much given to the admiration of Rimbaud, Verlaine and,
in general, the 'decadent' intellectual life grouped around the
French *café*, and attaching for my own part a high sentimental and
indeed a practical value to the social life of public houses, I felt
that the *Paris-Journal* columnist was not far wrong. The Catholics I frequented had a use even for English public houses, and
the last generation of their literary predecessors, especially G. K.
Chesterton, whom, it is true, they repudiated, had glorified beer.
Financially improvident as Bloy was, he clearly would not serve
as an apologist for mere Bohemianism.

I find, too, that my memory has played me an odd trick with
regard to *Le Pèlerin de l'Absolu*. For fifteen years I remained convinced that it was in this book that Bloy had expressed his curious pleasure in the fire which burned down the Opéra Comique
in 1887, a manifest improbability since *Le Pèlerin de l'Absolu* covers
only the years 1910-1912. Not but that *Le Pèlerin de l'Absolu*,
now that I look through it again, is sufficiently full of pleased re-
cording of disasters—crashing aviators, a train accident, the
Brussels exhibition, an explosion in the harbour at Toulon, the
'Titanic':

Millionaires have been drowned. An unheard-of luxury surrounded them, while, down in the hold, there existed a kind of hell for poor emigrants. I am sorry for them, but what else could I feel than the sweetest consolation when I think of the others? *Excandescet in illos aqua maris.*

Elsewhere, Bloy says that it was he who threw the iceberg which sank this unfortunate vessel. The fire at the Opéra Comique is mentioned only in *La Femme Pauvre*, of which I must have read the closing pages before I read the book as a whole. I could not, I felt, have rejoiced so openly, whoever was burnt. Bloy exulted at the 'suffocation or cremation' of so many (four hundred) 'unclean *bourgeois*', and thought it appropriate the disaster should have supervened upon 'the abject music of M. Ambroise Thomas'. It was a sign of the wrath to come, 'a light breath of the respiration of your God' — 'Him Who Burns'.

Le Désespéré was published in the year of that fire. Bloy was then turned forty. *Le Désespéré* tells the story of Caïn Marchenoir, his early life and conversion and his relations with a prostitute, Véronique, who, trembling on the verge of sainthood, goes mad. Caïn Marchenoir is Bloy himself, and Véronique also had an original. Marchenoir, troubled by his relations with Véronique, which he describes as a '*concubinage céleste*', makes a retreat at the Grande Chartreuse, is told by the abbot that he is without religious vocation and, returning to Paris, discovers that in order to destroy his passion for her, Véronique has caused all her teeth to be extracted and her hair cut off. This sublime action fails to produce the desired effect. Marchenoir's passion is, if anything, augmented. But he is stayed by the fact that Véronique becomes subject to visions in which the divine symbolism of history is revealed to them both. When she is eventually put away, he is run over on the way back from the asylum and dies without priest.

This story is less interesting than the course of events from which it was derived. Bloy's relation with the real-life Véronique, Anne-Marie Roulet, was a remarkable one. Whereas in *Le Désespéré* Marchenoir converts by inhumanly denying her, in real life he did not break off carnal relations until later and then went on living in spiritual intimacy with her. In the story, Véronique's madness comes too suddenly, and the episode of the teeth and hair is robbed of its pathos and made more ludicrous. All this does Bloy credit humanly. But Anne-Marie went on living at the Bon-Sauveur asylum on the outskirts of Paris until 1907. I do not know what visiting facilities were then granted at French asylums, and, with the exception of Carton de Wiart, Bloy's biographers are silent on the matter, but I have the impression that, although he continued to brood upon and to write about her, Anne-Marie, once locked up, lingered for twenty-five years without consolation from her lover and illuminate. Carton de Wiart, however, states that in 1890, just before his marriage, Bloy was still contributing to her upkeep.

Anne-Marie's visions are undoubted, and Bloy considered himself to be in possession of a religious secret of the highest importance. It appears to have taken the form of knowing what precise signs should precede the Day of Judgment, then imminent, and what part he should himself play in those proceedings, a part comparable with that of St John the Baptist. How much, in the winter of 1935-6, I was affected by this apocalyptical vision, I find it difficult to judge now. I did not precisely expect the Second Coming or, I think, the proximate end of the world. The expectation of cataclysmic change must always be a consolation to those ill-served by the present. I was impatient, but I did not know for what. The only hallucinatory states to which I was subject were approaching black-outs caused by physical inanition. It was the book's obsession with poverty which chiefly mattered to me—its view that poverty is divine, that Christ was above all the Poor Man.

This, and perhaps its diatribes against one particular type of the rich—successful men of letters. For Bloy, the more culpable mandarins of his day were Paul Bourget, Louis Veuillot, Catulle Mendès, François Coppée, Jean Richepin, Laurent Tailhade, Daudet, Maupassant, Huysmans and Zola. Predominantly, they were flirting Catholics, and at one time or another Bloy had enjoyed cordial relations with most of them. Two whom he continued to defend after their death, though in life he quarrelled even with them, were Barbey d'Aurevilly and Ernest Hello. He quarrelled, too, with Rémy de Gourmont, who later happily characterised his work as the result of a collaboration between St Thomas Aquinas and Gargantua. In *Le Désespéré*, Marchenoir attends a literary party, and there are bitter satirical portraits of most of these writers and others of whose names literary history bears no trace. I had better not say who were for me in 1935 the embodiments of literary evil triumphant. It is not so much that any of them are now my personal friends as that they have come to appear so much less unlovable than the representative figures of the generation which followed them.

I was to have been received on New Year's Day. After Christmas, Father D'Arcy being then in town, I signed a declaration of faith in Latin, adopted a baptismal name and arranged to present myself at Farm Street on the morning of January the 1st, for admission to the sacraments. After a sleepless night, I presented myself, but it was to say that I could not do this thing. There were too many doctrines I could not literally believe. I was also much travailed by a consideration which I have recently found stated, I would say, to perfection in the writings of Simone Weil, who refused baptism out of 'love for that which is outside the visible church'. For the church is not truly Catholic. It leaves the pagan world of antiquity and the other religious cultures of to-day without meaning. I felt, too, that its meaning for those inside was too highly generalised. Although it teaches the uniqueness of each soul, it allots only three possible destinations to all souls, with, in some cases, a roundabout route by way of Purgatory.

That was not the end of it. It was in the curious frame of mind of one still hoping to believe that I went on reading Bloy. Receiving from a publisher the sum of twenty-five pounds, I travelled successively to Paris, Strasbourg (I had been a student there) and Brussels, where I stayed in a state of exemplary destitution at the house of a kindly and trustful old body called, with an evident symbolic fitness, Mme Pardon, who lived, no less symbolically, in the Rue de la Limite. It was in Brussels that I bought and read *Le Sang du Pauvre*, the fullest and most explicit statement of Bloy's mysticism of poverty. It was there, I fancy, too, that I acquired a book on Bloy hostile to him, Ernest Seillière's.

There, too, I have always supposed, I bought and began to read *La Femme Pauvre*. My physical horror of the sacrament was increased by a series of windows in Ste Gudule. These depict a story of the middle ages, in which one John of Leuwen stole a ciborium of consecrated hosts and sold them to the Jews who, on Good Friday, chanted maledictions over them and pierced them with daggers. Blood appeared upon the transubstantiated bread.

The rest of the winter I spent at Pigotts with Eric Gill, whom I am inclined in retrospect to consider the most amiable and perhaps also the noblest soul I ever met. Seillière began to disintoxicate me of Bloy (but only began). He treats Bloy psychopathologically, seeing in his mysticism only inordinate will to power and an alliance of himself with God against the rest of the world. One of Gill's two gifted sons-in-law, René Hague, who was in revolt against the church, had already begun to speak of 'that old bore Léon Bloy', but I took this to be mere impatience with a growing cult.

'*Le Sang du Pauvre*', says Bloy, '*c'est l'argent*'. He sees a large part of the cosmic process in terms of a eucharistic cannibalism by which this blood is drunk and devoured. The blood of the rich, on the other hand, is 'a foetid pus exuded by the ulcers of Cain'. The rich man is a false poor man, whose peculiarly stinking rags strike fear into the hearts of the very stars. Money 'kills and vivifies like the Word'. When a coin is given to a beggar with a bad grace, it 'pierces the poor man's hand, falls, pierces the earth, makes holes in the suns, flies across the firmament and compromises the universe'. To such mysterious interrelatedness of persons and things Bloy affixes the term 'reversibility'—'equivalent in philosophy for the great dogma of the Communion of Saints'. In *The Double Image*, writing of Bloy in 1946, I implied that he had not, as Péguy did, 'distinguished clearly between poverty and destitution (*pauvreté* and *misère*)'. I now see, re-reading *Le Sang du Pauvre*, that this is not the case:

Poverty groups men together, Destitution isolates them, because poverty is of Jesus, destitution of the Holy Ghost.

Poverty is the Relative—privation of the superfluous. Destitution is the Absolute—privation of the necessary.

14

Poverty is crucified, Destitution is the Cross itself. Jesus bearing the Cross is Poverty bearing Destitution. Jesus upon the Cross is Poverty bleeding upon Destitution.

That is Bloy. Péguy, who was nevertheless much attracted by socialism, makes a similar distinction in terms less highly symbolised and then goes on to say that, while it is the first duty of man to rescue others from destitution, the condition of poverty is desirable and that the demand for equality is a bookish cry raised only by those ignorant of destitution.

Bloy and Péguy never met, though Bloy wrote to Péguy in 1906 and, in January 1916, moved into the house at Bourg-la-Reine which Péguy had left in order to join the French army two years earlier. Bloy clearly derived his *distinguo* from Péguy. The second brief paragraph in the passage quoted above first occurs in his diary as a comment on Péguy's article which he had just read and about which he sent his younger contemporary a fan letter. To Bloy, however, both *misère* and *pauvreté* are metaphysical, and mere social justice cannot touch them.

Those among the rich who are not wholly criminal can understand poverty, since they are themselves poor, in a sense; destitution they cannot understand. They may give alms, but they cannot deplete themselves. They sympathise melodiously with the sufferings of Jesus, but his Cross fills them with horror—the *reality* of his Cross! They must have it in bright lights and in gold, weightless and expensive, a thing to set off the bosom of some beautiful woman. . . She, lacking even the loyalty to give her body to the unfortunates whose appetite she inflames, will this evening display all she can of her white charnel-house meat, the jewels glistening upon her like worms, and cause fools to adore it, at some function devoted to what is known as charity.

The heroine of *La Femme Pauvre*, Clotilde, is sent by her step-father, the abominable Chapuis, to model for an artist, Pélopidas Gacougnol. To her and to Bloy, who speaks here in person, this is worse than prostitution or rather is the worst form of prostitution.

The lengthy passage in which he says so I read aloud and translated to Eric Gill. Alas, I can no longer recall what precisely his comment was, though I seem to remember it as unemphatic and a little embarrassed. Certainly, Gill's own attitude to the flesh was devoid of Jansenist gloom. In his books, he makes great play with the erotic analogies of mystical experience. In his letters and in his conversation, there was a candour and a freedom of expression one might think self-consciously indulged. For Gill, to delight in the bodies of women was itself a sign of religious grace.

Yet I am not sure that the attitudes to the flesh of Bloy and Gill were in fact radically opposed. I am certain that Gill would never have recommended sensuality without love. To Bloy, the body of a woman was a sanctuary and *Janua coeli*, the gate of Heaven, and for that reason he wished it veiled. There is a distinct vein of mystical eroticism in Bloy. It is thus expressed in a passage from the *Letters to His Fiancée* resumed almost word for word in *La Femme Pauvre*:

> Every woman, *whether she knows it or not*, is persuaded that her body is Paradise. *Plantaverat autem Dominus Deus Paradisum voluptatis a principio*, etc. (Genesis XI. 8.) Consequently no prayer, no penitence, no martyrdom has purchasing power enough to obtain this priceless jewel. The weight in gold of all the planets would not buy it. Judge what she gives when she gives herself, and then measure the sacrilege when she sells herself. . . A woman is RIGHT to believe all that and to affirm it with obstinacy. She is infinitely right because her body—that part of her body!—was the tabernacle of the living God.

When Bloy wrote *La Femme Pauvre*, he was already married. The view expressed by Albert Béguin is that Clotilde in the later part of the book is modelled upon Bloy's wife, Jeanne Molbech, daughter of a Danish poet, while in the earlier part she is Berthe Dumont, with whom Bloy lived in the bitter and rebellious period which followed upon the incarceration of Anne-Marie. *La Femme Pauvre* is a very much better novel than *Le Désespéré*,

16

though it, too, after the first few chapters, tends to be dissipated in argument and digression. It needs to be borne in mind, however, that Bloy initiated single-handed the Catholic novel as we understand it to-day. In the *Double Image*, I have indicated specific passages in the work of Mauriac and Bernanos which appear to me to be derived from him.

Clotilde Maréchal is thirty. She lives with her stepfather and her mother, who adores him. They have known prosperity, but what money they now have is spent on Chapuis's liquor and mother's *petites douceurs*. Clotilde has worked hard and fallen ill. She is of pure life, though she once yielded to a young man's importunities out of boredom and compassion. Once, when her mother was away, perhaps by arrangement, Chapuis tried to rape her, but she laid him out with one of the fire-irons. Feeling that she has reached the limit of degradation and that even modelling for an artist can no longer touch her, Clotilde presents herself at the house of Pélopidas Gacougnol. He, a jovial and foul-mouthed Gascon, has a visitor when she arrives and tells her to go behind a screen and undress. When the visitor has gone, Gacougnol hears the sound of weeping behind the screen and finds that his model, whom he had forgotten, has removed only one piece of clothing. His bark is worse than his bite, and, upon learning of her reluctance to expose her person to him, he decides that he can paint her clothed as a martyr in the arena and takes her off to the zoo with him to sketch lions. There they meet Caïn Marchenoir, who explains to Clotilde what part animals play in the universal scheme. He insists that the animals suffer not only through but for man. Clotilde questions whether this view is consistent with divine justice, since animals die without hope of salvation.

You would like to know what their reward is and how they are paid. If I knew and could tell you, mademoiselle, I should be God, for then I should know what the animals are *in themselves* and not merely in their relation to man. You must have observed how we perceive things only in their relations with each other, never in their ground and in their essence. No man can affirm with confidence that any perceptible form is indelible or bears within it an eternal character. We sleep, . . . and we dream the outside world, seeing it as in a glass darkly. We shall not understand this vale of tears until all its secrets are revealed to us. . . Till that time, we must accept, ignorant as sheep, the spectacle of universal sacrifice, repeating to ourselves that suffering, if it were not shrouded in mystery, could neither enlist martyrs by its beauty and power nor merit its endurance by animals.

Gacougnol, seeing how important it is for Clotilde that she should be removed from her squalid surroundings, sets her up in honourable lodgings of her own. Her mother attempts to blackmail him. Clotilde meets and marries Léopold, a draughtsman and friend of Marchenoir's. Marchenoir addresses to them a sombre epithalamion. Every minute, a hundred persons die and a hundred are born. In one hour of their wedding night, six thousand corpses accumulate beneath the nuptial bed. For in this reversible world the joy of lovers must be paid. In order that two people may briefly separate themselves from the suffering world, suffering elsewhere must be increased. At the very moment at which she 'bleats with pleasure', Clotilde will hear beyond the walls of her room the wailing and gnashing of teeth of the man who had no wedding garment and was cast into outer darkness.

Marchenoir dies. Clotilde and Léopold live in extreme poverty. Léopold is killed rescuing victims of the fire at the Opéra Comique. Clotilde lives on to affirm that 'everything which happens calls for adoration' and to conclude: '*Il n'y a qu'une tristesse. . . c'est de* N'ÊTRE PAS DES SAINTS' . . . 'That we are not saints is the only thing that ought properly to sadden us.'

I wrote articles on Bloy for two quarterlies since defunct, *Purpose* and T. S. Eliot's *Criterion*. In the one, I contrasted Bloy's 'gift of tears' with Keats's 'negative capability', Bloy being conspicuously one who could not 'live in uncertainties, mysteries, doubts, without any irritable reaching after reason and fact'. In *The Criterion* I attempted a synthesis between Bloy's cult of poverty and the requirements of social revolution. In the same article, I sketched out the view elaborated ten years later in *The Double*

Image that Christianity stands in radical opposition to the creative imagination and that a Christian writer of any power will necessarily tend towards a heresy. In Bloy I diagnosed Manichaeism of the usual kind and a Zoroastrian polarity of rich and poor, Christ personifying the one and some unnamed demiurge the other. These two were, I fancy, the first pieces on Bloy by a non-Catholic writing in English. That year, Messrs Sheed & Ward brought out a version of Barbara Wall's translation of *Lettres à sa Fiancée* and *La Femme Pauvre*. It seems that neither book was successful in English. In France, books on Bloy and previously unpublished writings of his continued to appear.

My article for *Purpose* must have been written before I went to Eric Gill's, that for the *Criterion* between Gill's and my next departure, to a derelict mansion James Hanley had bought in Merionethshire. That would be April, 1936. Other works by Léon Bloy which I had then read without feeling myself particularly marked by them would be *Le Salut par les Juifs*, *Dans les Ténèbres*, *Celle Qui Pleure*, *La Vie de Mélanie* and the two volumes of *Exégèse des Lieux Communs*. What else I knew about Bloy would have been derived from the books of Pierre Termier, Hubert Colleye, Stanislas Fumet and Léopold Levaux, an article in *Blackfriars* by Richard Kehoe, O.P., and the communications of Bernard Kelly, who by now, however, was beginning to complain that Bloy was temperamentally overcharged and that Kierkegaard was the man. To him, in any case, the La Salette books (*Celle Qui Pleure*, *La Vie de Mélanie* and *Le Symbolisme de l'Apparition*) had meant most. He was then engaged upon an intellectual task which he described as translating Karl Marx into the Latin of St Thomas Aquinas.

Religious inquietude thrives best in the winter, and I travelled to north Wales without very much of it. I ate regularly, and I enjoyed the pagan company of Hanley himself and John Cowper Powys, his neighbour. What I carried away from Gill's was a sense of the beauty of the liturgical year, a less erratic and more openly significant counterpoint to the seasons. These were inconspicuous in the writings of Léon Bloy. With him, it seemed always winter. Béguin, it is true, detects a seasonal rhythm in Bloy's religious life. He points to an annual prostration at Easter, followed by a powerful and creative summer. Béguin deplores any attempt to relate this cycle to the course of the sun and considers that it was the Passion which ravaged Bloy in early spring (may it not rather have been reminders of the terrible Easter during which he and Anne-Marie Roulet together looked for a sign?) and the festivals of the Virgin which revived him in summer. On the other hand, in *Letters to His Fiancée*, Bloy writes: 'The month of March is coming, the month of St Joseph whom I love so much, so let us be hopeful.' Yet he was city-pent. The family holidays he took in later life were generally purgatorial to him, at best a waste of time.

When Clotilde and Léopold go to live in the outer suburbs in *La Femme Pauvre*, Bloy comments on the middle-class attitude to trees.

Apart from the acacias and the scorched planes in the high street, you would have looked in vain for a decent tree in what had once been woodland. One of the most characteristic signs of the *petit bourgeois* is his hatred of trees. A frenzied, watchful hatred surpassed only by his well-known loathing for the stars and the imperfect subjunctive. Trembling with rage, he tolerates only fruit-trees, those which *bring something in* (*ceux qui rapportent*), and then only on condition that these unfortunate vegetable growths cling humbly to the walls and do not shade the kitchen garden, for the *petit bourgeois* likes the sun. It is the one star he patronises.

Yet neither for the stars themselves nor for trees (whose fruitfulness is not their least engaging quality, after all) are there many signs in Bloy's work that he entertained any but a symbolic and rhetorical regard. In 1906, in the forest of Eu, he says: '*Je suis un sylvestre.*' In 1911, he calls trees '*les plus belles oeuvres de Dieu*' and deplores the ability of some '*ignoble propriétaire*' to lay low '*une avenue d'arbres magnifiques dont la vue nous enchantait*'. Yet chiefly, we feel, he valued both trees and stars because they were not worldly priests, the rich or men of letters. The passage quoted above may even have been a literary echo of Stendhal, who, in *Le Rouge et le Noir*, complains of the trimmed plane-trees of Verrières.

'I like shade,' said M. de Rénal. . ., 'I prune *my* trees to give shade, and I don't see what other use trees have, unless they're really useful like walnuts and *bring something in. . . Je ne conçois pas qu'un arbre soit fait pour autre chose, quand toutefois. . . il ne rap-porte pas de revenu.*'

That summer, I was for my own part immersed in nature. The news on the wireless was of Italian Catholics blasting their way through Abyssinia (Father D'Arcy had shown me an Abys-sinian Madonna, brought him, I seem to remember, by Evelyn Waugh). I cut down trees, shot rabbits, played piano duets with Hanley, attended the local *eisteddfod*, where, to his enormous pleasure, they made Powys a bard, and wrote abortively at a novel. I was temporarily reconciled with Middleton Murry and lived at his Adelphi Centre for several months, during which I was also reconciled with George Orwell, who came down there to lecture, along with intellectual giants like Reinhold Niebuhr and men of subtle and compassionate mind like John Macmurray. I somehow found myself on the executive committee of the International Association for the Defence of Culture.

Winter had come on again. There appeared, in Karl Pfleger's *Wrestlers with Christ*, the first book in English containing an ac-count of Léon Bloy. I was still in the process of struggling free of the church and of attempting a synthesis between those elements of Catholicism which attracted me and that Revolu-tion we tended in those days to personify without attaching any very detailed meaning to it, one result of which confusion of mind has been a disappointment keen enough to turn some of the fellow-travellers of the 'thirties into diehard Tories. There was also to be worked into the synthesis what I valued in the pacifism recently embraced by Murry and more perfectly em-bodied by the Quaker-trained Max Plowman. I put my uncert-ainties into the form of a series of propositions, which I sent round to various people I knew, asking for comment, and subsequently published in *The Adelphi*. They appear with Max Plowman's reply in the huge volume of his letters called *Bridge into the Future*.

I suggested that ours was 'still a Christocentric universe', that

21

the psychoanalysts were wrong in supposing the cult of the Blessed Virgin Mary to be a sublimated Oedipus complex (that, on the contrary, 'the incest motive' was 'a sign that men are lost without Our Lady, without Immaculate Conception and Virgin Birth, and so must seek to overcharge their mothers and sisters, their mistresses and wives, too, with a supernatural passion'), that mere humanism was metaphysically inadequate but that, 'on the other hand, the Aristotelian universe of Roman Catholicism allows no meaningful reality to Man', that there was 'dangerously much in common to communism and fascism', that, while communism might be necessary and while it might even be our duty to affirm it over against *bourgeois* capitalism, yet in itself it merely 'continued the tradition of accumulation and enclosure', and that:

> The Bourgeois, the Enemy, is above all the principle of inertia and accumulation, the absolutely unloving man, enclosure, security, the man who will not pray, fearing the nakedness, the vulnerability, the giving the show away, of love. And reducing any giant equation of joy and pain to its smallest equivalent factors of pleasure and anxiety.

Among 'possible true prophets', I listed Plato, Dionysius the Areopagite, Gregory of Nyssa, Augustine, Blake, Léon Bloy and Berdyaev. During that winter, the atmosphere at the Adelphi Centre, with its conflicting purposes and tangle of personal relationships (reminiscent at once of *Wuthering Heights* and *Cold Comfort Farm*), was so tense one half expected the building itself to levitate or burst into flames, there in the heart of the Essex countryside. At the beginning of 1937, I left.

I married, with Herbert Read and Max Plowman as the two witnesses, and went to live in Hampstead. It was, I suppose, reasonably certain by now that I had escaped conversion. About the Spanish war I had some acerbities with Father D'Arcy. Those born too late will realise with difficulty how churned up English intellectual life was by the war in Spain. With a very few exceptions, of which Ezra Pound and Roy Campbell were the chief (with Edmund Blunden and T. S.

Eliot almost the only neutrals), those writers to whom one gave any thought were unanimously on the side of the republican government. Catholics generally tended the other way. The Jesuits and those whom they influenced were crying crusade for all they were worth. The Dominicans (and those whom *they* influenced, like E. I. Watkin and Eric Gill) behaved more judiciously and were inclined to a pacifist view. In France, Georges Bernanos and Jacques Maritain came out heavily, if not on the government side, at any rate against Franco's falangists and Moors, to say nothing of the German and Italian intervention. At first torn and trying hard to belong to the neutrals, I was borne irresistibly leftward. It was some time before George Orwell came home with his proofs that we were not faced with anything like the straightforward alignment of a football match, that the political minorities fighting on the government side were being callously exterminated by Stalinist party-liners. I was deflected again towards a pacifism in which I was greatly confirmed by the reports of Sir Richard Rees, who had been out driving ambulances with Julian Bell. In the end, one felt little but pity and the fear of what the right-wing press continued to assure us was not going to happen elsewhere in Europe.

I had felt unhappily certain where Bloy's sympathies would have lain. Perhaps wrongly? What I regarded as his simple-minded reactions to the 1914 war in *Dans les Ténèbres* appeared to me to be of the type which had brought Claudel out as a crusader and were to lead him presently to welcome Pétain. An American of French extraction, writing about my *Criterion* article, thought I had missed the whole point about Bloy and that he was essentially a disappointed patriot. This did not appear to me to be the case. Or rather, it appeared to me that his disappointment had been a mere incident of his adolescence. The rich against whom he later directed his animosity were, after all, French rich. On the other hand, he had been in arms against the Commune in 1871, and it was during the Franco-Prussian war that he first received what appeared to him to be a mystical revelation.

Two poems I wrote in 1937 directly paraphrase or make play with ideas from Léon Bloy. One elaborates a remarkable passage on the crucifixion in *Le Salut par les Juifs*. Another introduces 'the coin on the hand of the beggar' in *Le Sang du Pauvre*. A third, written in a mood of almost blissful fatalism just before the outbreak of war in 1939, recurs to 'silver the blood of the poor in a ring of rain' – the 'ring of rain' having to do with medieval conjuration of demons and not with Léon Bloy. But after 1937 I read no more Bloy until I had to look up certain passages again for *The Double Image*, so that, until I began to write this essay, I had gone fourteen years without effective intercourse with his work, or only the intercourse of memory. Towards the end of 1949, I had the notion that too much reading in a foreign language is bad for a writer, since he begins to think in that language and to lose command of his own, which is his firm rock. Apart from a few works of philosophy and the classics which I fancied requisite to the schooling of my children, I therefore sold all my French books – except those of Bloy and of one other writer, Marcel Jouhandeau.

On the 19th of September, 1846, at La Salette-Fallavaux, about fifty miles south-east of Grenoble, the Virgin Mary appeared in tears to a boy and a girl tending cows on the mountain-side. She told them that the wickedness of this world and the indifference of the church caused her actual suffering and that the time was almost come when she could no longer restrain the heavy arm of her son from striking. Mélanie Calvat was fifteen years old, Maximin Giraud eleven. Their accounts of the apparition, taken down the following day by their employer, were circumstantial and verisimilitudinous. Pilgrims visited the place. Ecclesiastical opinion was divided. Mélanie Calvat, whose childhood had been one of exceptional hardship, was questioned repeatedly by the clergy and, in the course of her fairly long life, dictated or composed more than one detailed narrative of her experience, each highly consonant with the rest. She died a nun in Italy. A church was set up on the site, with accommodation for pilgrims.

Bloy first visited La Salette in his early thirties, during his 'Véronique' period. He was currently under the influence of the well-to-do Abbé Tardif de Moidrey, who had proposed that they should subsequently travel together to the Holy Land, but died only a few days after Bloy's return to Paris. The apocalyptical threats contained in the 'secret' of Mélanie naturally appealed to Bloy. Much given to the discovery of symbolism in what to other people would seem coincidence, he also attached importance to the fact that the apparition had taken place in the year of his own birth, which was also the year of the birth of Anne-Marie, and that between the date of his birth and the date of the apparition there had elapsed sixty-eight days, 'the number of the brothers of the faithful Obededom chosen with him by King David to be the guardians of the Ark of the Covenant'. One is reminded of Blake, who, at the age of thirty-three, dated from the year of his own birth the advent of a 'new heaven'. There do in fact seem to have been sixty-eight clear days between the day on which Bloy was born and the day on which the apparition was seen. On other occasions, however, Bloy procured a different symbolism by working the sum out differently, even fudging the date of his birth by a day.

On his second visit to La Salette with Anne-Marie, Bloy was asked to leave by the brethren, who failed to perceive the sublimity of his relations with the lady by whom he was accompanied. This, to Bloy, was a further proof that the true significance of the apparition was being ignored, and he began work on *Le Symbolisme de l'Apparition*, which he did not complete to his own satisfaction and which remained unpublished until eight years after his death. In 1907, however, he published *Celle Qui Pleure*, and in 1911 he edited a life of Mélanie Calvat written by herself and prefaced it with an introduction which is among his finest writings. Perhaps oddly, he never visited or, until it was too late, showed a desire to visit Mélanie herself, who lived on to the end of 1904.

The *jeunesses* of Mélanie are moving in the extreme and full of that bitter charm of the folk-imagination we know best through the *Märchen* collected by the Brothers Grimm. To this, Bloy was or allowed himself to appear insensitive, though he was not slow to insist upon the unmerited sufferings and the poverty of this child sold by her parents and brutalised by her first masters into a strange taciturnity and inwardness, so that she

25

became known locally as '*la Louve*' - 'the she-wolf'. From the age of three, she was accompanied in her solitude by a mysterious brother, who upon occasion performed miracles and who promised her a loving mother, her own mother having from the cradle treated her with a morbid spite.

She saw and felt *in* God. She had to pass, so to say, through God, to pierce through a threefold partition of light, to reach things sensible, as hard to distinguish for her as a labourer's poor belongings when he comes home dazzled by the glare of the sun in the fields at harvest-time.

This image may seem to belie what I have already said about Léon Bloy and nature, but it is unique in his work.
He proceeds quickly to his astonishing doctrine.

Jesus sprang from Mary as Adam did from the earthly Paradise, to obey and to suffer. Mary is therefore expressed in the Garden of Delight 'planted by God in the beginning'. The second chapter of *Genesis* is quite incomprehensible if we do not keep Mary in mind.

The four rivers comprise the vocation of Mary, and 'no spirit can receive God but through Mary, just as the Son of God could not be born except by the operation in Her of the Holy Spirit'. The horror of the centuries and the insufficiency of the redemption through Christ forced, metaphysically, the apparition at La Salette, an apparition even then incomplete, since it required also the apparition to Bernadette Soubirous at Lourdes twelve years later and the curious appearances in the sky at Pontmain during the Franco-Prussian war. To La Salette, however, Lourdes was

a *travesty* of your grief, an impersonation, such as might be played by a mother who, with death at her heart, should put on her best dress in order not to frighten the children.

There was a gap of twenty-five years in Bloy's active devotion to Notre Dame de la Salette. His first expectations were coupled not only with his hopes of the Abbé Tardif de Moidrey but also with Anne-Marie's insistence that Easter, 1880, should not go by without a sign. The inevitable disappointment closely preceded and may have precipitated Anne-Marie's final madness, which for some months jolted Bloy out of his religious faith. *Celle Qui Pleure* was not written until the year of Anne-Marie's death. The divine meaning of historical events remained, nevertheless, Bloy's constant study. Marie-Antoinette, Christopher Columbus, Louis XVII, Joan of Arc, Napoleon and the fire at the Opéra Comique appeared in turn to him as vehicles of exceptional light. In the perspective of divine history, a special importance attached to the Jews.

Le Salut par les Juifs appeared in 1892. The date is all-important. The Dreyfus affair did not flare up until two years later. France was the last of the European countries to fall a prey to political anti-Semitism, which, as Bloy pointed out much later to an unknown lady correspondent, is 'a thing peculiar to modern times', a conscious and deliberated revival of what in the middle ages sprang more innocently from other roots. If we except the further revival under Hitler, the whole epidemic lasted only thirty-two years, though its grumbling undertones remain even in England, which never disgraced itself in this respect. Beginning with Germany in 1873, it spread over Russia, Austria-Hungary and Turkey. In the European countries, it originated in the attempt to find a scapegoat for economic crisis, and at least in its initial stages it always received papal blessing. In France, the financial scandal which started it was the Panama crash. In 1882, Paul Bontoux founded the Union Générale, a Catholic and legitimist organisation for breaking the alleged Jewish and Protestant stranglehold on business. The text-book of the movement, *La France Juive* by Edouard Drumont, equivalent in France of Wilhelm Marr's *Sieg des Judenthums über das Germanthum*, appeared in 1886, and in 1892 Drumont started his anti-Semitic daily paper, *La Libre Parole*. The army and the clergy were solidly behind him, and such titled hooligans as the Comte de Lamase and the Marquis

27

de Morès whipped up street-terror and provoked the more prominent Jews to fight duels.

The real nature of Bloy's response to this situation is not easy to formulate. That he was repelled by the Drumont campaign and recognised the ignoble motives behind it, we may well believe. *Le Salut par les Juifs*, however, is anything but a humanitarian defence of the Jews. Indeed, with regard to the Jews of his own time, Bloy seems to grant Drumont all his points. Clearly, he was not one to fall for the notion that shady finance is exclusively Jewish or that only the Jews are rich. He was, at the same time, or had been a legitimist, and we must remember that the term '*bourgeois*' still faintly connoted liberalism and anti-clericalism in politics and religion. One of his benefactors, Mme Charles Hayem, had been a Jewess. It was she who had paid for his second pilgrimage to La Salette, and on that occasion he had written to her that

> Israel is the ancestor of us Catholics, and those who do not honour him are threatened by the scriptures themselves with short life. I regret to see Catholics frequently ignore so evident a truth.

Yet there is no indication that, at the time of writing *Le Salut par les Juifs*, Bloy honoured Israel other than metaphysically. On the human level, the utmost he is willing to concede is that it is not so wicked for Jews as it is for Frenchmen to be rich and that the middle ages had properly abandoned the practice of usury and commerce to the Jews.

Metaphysically, too, there is contradiction. '*Jésus sera en agonie jusqu'à la fin du monde*', said Pascal. That is the fault of the Jews. Their rejection has, so to say, frozen the redemptive process. When they believe, Jesus will be able to come down from the cross. Till then, the events of Good Friday are repeated endlessly through time. Pilate is still washing his hands, Peter still awaiting cock-crow. Darkness covers the earth. Yet the crime of the Jews does not deprive them of their position as a chosen people. Money is not only the blood of the poor. It is also the word of God, which came from the Jews both as a

written word and as the incarnate Word. The Jews have crucified money. They have raised it up on high, isolating the blood
of the poor from the poor. But they are themselves the cross,
which is the Holy Ghost and from which in the end the Word
must come down. Mary, the bride of the Holy Ghost, was and
is a Jewess. The Holy Ghost is the Messiah for whom the Jews
are still criminally and yet in a sense rightly waiting.

At the human level, Bloy became increasingly confused. In
1894, the year in which Dreyfus was condemned and sent to
Devil's Island, he wrote to a young Danish Catholic advising her
not to marry a Jewish convert, and, visiting Barbey d'Aurevilly's grave, he was appalled by the proximity of the Jewish
cemetery. Dreyfus was brought back and 'pardoned' five years
later. Zola's article, '*J'Accuse*', had appeared in *L'Aurore* the
previous year. Zola, brought to trial and condemned to a year's
imprisonment, had taken refuge in England. Bloy hated Zola
and wrote against him a book, *Je M'Accuse*, which had the
misfortune not to appear until after Dreyfus had been set at
liberty. Zola was not the only Dreyfusard of Bloy's acquaintance.
There was also Clemenceau, and there was Henry de Groux, to
whom Bloy wrote during Dreyfus's second trial that he prayed
daily at communion that God would quickly decide the case
one way or the other. In *Je M'Accuse*, he says that, 'despite the in-
famy of those who defend him', he is convinced of the innocence
of Dreyfus in the sense that on Devil's Island he is expiating
somebody else's crime, but that God does not permit meaningless suffering, so that Dreyfus must be guilty of another crime,
probably connected with the fact that he is rich. 'What was the
origin of his wealth, and what use did he make of it?' Mere
human justice is of no account. The opposition of Jew and
Christian is outside time. The Jew is the elder brother who turns
away when the fatted calf is killed for the prodigal. And now
here are the Jews allied with the Protestants, which is monstrous.

What in fact is Protestantism but the waste matter of Christianity, the negation of Essence and revealed Substance?
When a man says, 'I am a Protestant!' it is as though he
were to say, 'I do not exist!'

In the end, Bloy tried to sum up his position by saying that he was not and did not wish to be either Dreyfusard or anti-Dreyfusard or anti-Semite. He was simply anti-swine and in that sense against practically everybody.

Le Salut par les Juifs remained out of print for twelve years. In 1905, Dreyfus, pardoned and set at liberty six years earlier, secured his demand for the third trial which fully rehabilitated him. The scandal of his first trial had so damaged the church in the eyes of the people that its disestablishment in France had become inevitable. Bloy had now made, in Raïssa Maritain, a Jewess, one of his most distinguished converts. He dedicated the second edition to her, and it is in this dedication that he says that his book was never more than exegetical paraphrase of the eleventh chapter of St Paul's epistle to the Romans.

Now if the fall of them be the riches of the world, and the diminishing of them the riches of the Gentiles, how much more their fulness?. . . If the casting away of them be the reconciling of the world, what shall the receiving of them be, but life from the dead?

Here, too, he insists not only on the earthly Jewishness of Christ, for

the Blood poured out on the cross for the Redemption of mankind, like that which daily flows unseen in the Chalice of the Sacrament at the Altar, is naturally and supernaturally *Jewish blood,*

while in the letter already quoted he affirms that

Anti-Semitism. . . is the most horrible injury Our Lord has received in the course of his continuing Passion; it is a buffet outrageous and unforgivable, since he receives it *on the face of his Mother* and from Christian hands.

It may be recalled here that Georges Bernanos, in many ways admirable and in some ways a successor to Bloy, was in this matter less free of the toxin and that the spirit of Drumont for a time revived in him, as it did with greater virulence in the author of *A Journey to the End of the Night*. Towards Dreyfus himself Bloy maintained the hostility one may feel for a disturber of the peace whose cause is not one's own. Upon his final rehabilitation in 1906, Bloy noted in his diary:

I require no further proof of this man's guilt than his acceptance of these favours, manifestly designed to outrage the French soul.

These favours were military promotion and an award of the Legion of Honour.

With even a trace of true feeling in him, he would have rejected them and taken refuge in the deepest obscurity.

After Mélanie Calvat and the Jews, Napoleon played the chief part in Bloy's providential drama of history, and it is here that my American correspondent was perhaps most nearly right about the importance of the patriotic element in Bloy, though I feel that in fact Napoleon represented, as he did for Stendhal, an adolescent fixation and that Bloy's attempt to integrate him into the redemptive scheme was forced. Napoleon was a pagan hero of Bloy's youth, whom, after his own conversion, he would have liked to convert.

L'Ame de Napoléon was written at the age of sixty-five. As much of Napoleon as the main theme will accommodate appears already in *Le Sang du Pauvre*. In middle life, Bloy disapproved of Napoleon as, for instance, the man who had set himself to abolish poverty. At the same time, from the depths of his youth, fascination and hero-worship well up, and there are diary entries in which he says that 'at the very name of Napoleon' his heart 'breaks with love, as if it were the name of God', or that he has this great man so much in his blood that he 'can hardly hear him mentioned' without having his equilibrium in some way 'upset or restored', or that to read about Napoleon catches his breath and almost causes him to sob as though God were passing. One might suspect that, as for many a poor lunatic,

31

Napoleon remained for Bloy the only person whose incomprehensible otherness he had ever fully acknowledged, his recognition yet tinged with megalomania from the beginning.

It is indeed the very stupor with which one is filled by contemplation of Napoleon's career that seemed to Bloy to be his meaning. Napoleon prefigures the reign of the Holy Ghost. It is even possible to say that Providence will need to imitate Napoleon's strategy. Yet worse must first come. Napoleon had not the perfection of evil required of Antichrist. He was all-too-human both in his weaknesses and in his magnanimity towards his enemies. And here Bloy is led to what is at once the more psychologically suspect and the more commonplace part of his thesis, for Napoleon himself he portrays as the lonely man surrounded by creatures of unbelievable mediocrity.

Napoleon's meaning, however, transcends Napoleon. His coronation may be envisaged 'as a form of extreme unction administered to a dying Europe'.

> History is like an immense liturgical text. . . What is known as Genius is simply the divine Will incarnate, if I may put it so, made visible and tangible in a human instrument brought to its highest degree of force and precision, incapable, however, like a pair of compasses, of going beyond its own greatest circumference.

In the journal he kept while he was writing *L'Ame de Napoléon*, Bloy says that Napoleon was so great that world rule was a mere *pis-aller* for him. At the same time, it is difficult not to feel the force of an objection raised by one of Bloy's correspondents, that 'from the point of view of faith, it is evident that you could write the equally supernatural history of any other soul, even that of a bailiff'. Bloy's retort is facetious: 'No doubt, my dear Borrel, but where would you find the soul of a bailiff?' Yet in fact he implies himself that it is so. 'All men are symbolic', he says, 'and it is in the measure of his symbol that each man lives'. The battle of Friedland might equally well have been won 'by a little girl of three or a centenarian tramp begging God that his Will should be done on earth as it is in Heaven'.

We are, all of us, expressions of the Invisible and . . . you cannot lift a finger or massacre two million men without indicating what shall be manifest only in the beatific Vision.

Bloy's hatred of the English is connected both with his admiration for Napoleon and with his view of the mission of the Jews. The nullity of Protestantism may be seen elsewhere. In Denmark, the only foreign country in which Bloy spent more than a few hours, he considered that three and a half centuries of Lutheran darkness had turned the people imbecile. Germany he remembered chiefly as the enemy of 1870. England, however, had also been Napoleon's enemy. We may think that this was a long time ago. We may also think that, granting Bloy his premises, it was perhaps the divine mission of England to defeat Napoleon. At one point in his journals, Bloy seems prepared to admit the silliness of historical feuds. Generally, his humour was satirical, destructive and too heavily charged with significance. Occasionally, however, he betrays a merely human smile, as when, writing in hot weather upon the apparition at La Salette, he notes down the temperature and adds, 'Celle Qui Pleure *par celui qui sue*', or in the epilogue to *Léon Bloy devant les Cochons*, when, his ill humour voided, he delightfully begs the pardon of all four-footed pigs. In February, 1908, he records that:

A French painter has been naturalised English. 'Why did you do that?' he is asked. Reply: 'Before, I had lost the battle of Waterloo. Now I have won it.'

Bloy silently registers a hit. For once, he does not characterise the painter as '*gâteux*', '*imbécile*', '*goujat*', '*sot*', '*cuistre*', '*lâcheur*' or '*renégat*'. Normally, however, his view is that 'England is to the world what the Devil is in the life of man'. She was the land of the rich, and she was ruled by a queen who was not the Queen of Heaven. In his diary for 1894, Bloy notes that he has just read a book on Freemasonry in England and that it is very badly written but full of a salutary and refreshing hatred of the English race.

33

These fifteen or twenty years, I have nursed the same thought, the same vision. I still *see* a victorious army of a million men surrounding London: – Let all who love Mary, *Mary bleeding*, and the white Vicar of Christ *come and join us*, and then let twenty thousand of the most powerful pieces of ordnance thunder tirelessly and without mercy upon this city of the damned until nothing remains of it but an immense heap of dust.

The author of this very sensible but perhaps not altogether kindly thought had never set foot in England, nor can I recall any indication that he had met an Englishman before the end of September, 1914, when British troops appeared at Le Mans and were found to have '*la plus belle allure du monde.*' Palm Sunday in 1900 was also the birthday of the Danish king, Christian IX.

His ignoble son-in-law, the Prince of Wales, is in Copenhagen, an attempt to assassinate him at the Gare du Nord in Paris having failed. A young Belgian shot at the swine and missed. Swine are supposed to be bled. It is more efficacious, and the blood is needed for black pudding.

There are several equally gracious references to Queen Victoria. Upon the outbreak of the Boer war, Bloy rejoiced to see the nations unite in condemnation of England. There was hope yet. He also blamed England for the introduction of compulsory vaccination into France.

It is 1951. At the end of a rather poor summer, the weather is turning cold. The newspapers are full of Persian oil, suspended truce-talks in Korea and the endless succession of crimes, disasters, whimsies and success-stories which apparently make up the modern world. The streets of London jump day and night with traffic, but, as windows close, the wireless nuisance is a little abated. Upon my shelves, the space devoted to Bloy in red buckram has become much disordered. From the International Book Club, I have the first three previously unread volumes.

34

I approach Bloy now with fascination, painful nostalgia and a variety of other emotions among which I cannot fail to detect an element of distaste. What I remember I remember vividly. What I have still to read will, I know, seem only too familiar. The world has changed, and my attitude to it has changed. Just after the war, I was writing, in *The Double Image*, that there is a sense in which every European is a practising Christian.

Even the Germans have not succeeded in wiping the slate of the mind clean of its Christian attitudes and dispositions. The European languages are of Christian formation. Our codes of law, our domestic customs, are Christian. The modern world has not yet found a new centre for itself. Until it does, this is still a Christocentric world, and Europe is Christendom.

It is not yet wholly untrue. A certain amount of religious instruction is still given in British primary schools. A large industry flourishes in connection with ecclesiastical buildings and Christian burial customs. England is officially a Christian country, and the clergy exercise a political influence throughout western Europe and in the Americas. One is nevertheless more conscious of the world not having yet found a new centre for itself than of what centre there is being still the figure of Christ or in any other sense Christian.

I turn the pages of Termier, Colleye, Fumet and Martineau and see repeated the four or five photographs and the two self-portraits of a man with popping eyes and an enormous moustache. '*Un Bismarck calamiteux*', Paul Bourget called him. Here, there is a look of Nietzsche, but the features are less fine. Another photograph reveals that there was a similar lack of back to the head in both men. Admiring critics who write about Bloy from personal knowledge describe only his old age, growing in serenity, yet not wholly free of petulance, vanity and wild accusation. In 1911, he stands amid his family in a narrow courtyard in Montmartre. His wife, considerably taller than himself, lean and fair, has a Mongol cast of features. The younger daughter, Madeleine, solemnly clutching her violin, takes after her mother. Véronique, sitting in front with a guitar, dark, plump and loose-mouthed, stares at the camera-man with anything but a spiritual expression. Bloy is stocky and dignified, his white moustache now drooping. Here, in 1887, the eyes are hypnotic. One would not have been surprised to find that they were the eyes of a theosophist or a murderer. It would certainly not have been one's first guess that they were those of an important writer.

Perhaps they were not. That is what I have to determine if I can. I must first attempt to characterise the personality associated with that face (Bloy himself was of the opinion that a writer's works ought to show in his face). Whether it was a sufficiently distinct and interesting personality will then no doubt appear. A writer's importance can only be discussed under necessarily artificial schematic heads. We may distinguish between a purely literary importance and the importance of a message. We may withhold both from a writer and yet grant him a prototypical significance. In the case of a writer attached like Bloy to a religious institution, it will be necessary to distinguish his institutional importance from his importance to those outside. For it has to be admitted that there is a Catholic literature, whose products are of no interest to the rest of us unless we happen to be studying Catholicism. That Bloy is a surprising oddity has perhaps appeared already. That he enjoyed the primary literary importance of a superlatively good writer of French prose has been asserted on behalf of Jacques Maritain, a Catholic himself, but one who has found means of appealing to readers outside the church. That kind of assertion is in any case one which only a Frenchman is entitled to make. It is not my belief that a foreigner can pronounce valid judgement on the intimate detail of any play with language.

Part Two

All his life, Léon Bloy exhibited symptoms of persecution mania and other recognised forms of psychosis. He did not succumb to them. On the contrary, despite his privations, he lived to the exemplary age of seventy-one in full possession of his faculties. This is perhaps the central fact about his personality. Moreover, although at the inferior level of psychopathology, he betrayed frequent signs of coprophilia, sado-masochism and narcissism, he seems to have contrived, from the age of forty-four onwards, to enjoy a happy relationship of marriage.

A robust physical constitution Bloy must have had. A limit there must nevertheless have been to his privations. He must—not to put too fine a point on it—have eaten rather better than he gives out. Two sons died in childhood. There were days of complete fast. Yet Bloy brought up two daughters. His widow lived to a ripe age. There was no history of chronic disease in the family. The effects of malnutrition are one of the studies most emphatically advanced by the last war. We in England have developed a national hypochondria by thinking about them. There is no indication that they were exhibited by Léon Bloy. We are forced to regard his rather as a life of misery in the English sense than of *misère* in the French. He lived in some poverty and was at moments destitute. Physically, the *régime* evidently suited him. A recurrent note throughout his journals is struck by entries in which he records the demise of one after another of his well-to-do enemies and rivals.

Bloy's attitude to his circumstances varied. He tells us repeatedly that he prayed in early manhood to be granted suffering. He shows a good deal of insight when a disciple leaves him or a benefactor withdraws or an editor decides to accept no more articles from him. He will not relax his posture of total defiance. Bloy in fact maintained a primary, untempted integrity. A full acceptance of his position and its consequences was nevertheless beyond him. He did not flinch, but he frequently complained. In a recent work, Joseph Bollery, quite unsuspectingly, places together letters written by Bloy at an interval of a few days, in one of which he thanks his publisher for pecuniary aid and in the other, written to Théodore de Banville, states that his publisher does nothing for him and that he is absolutely without bread. It is all very well, too, for a man to attach to himself as a *titre de gloire* a name – 'the ungrateful beggar' – first given him derogatively. One is nevertheless shocked when he writes to Pierre Termier that he is called 'Termier' *because* he is destined to pay Bloy's '*terme*' – his rent. One is perhaps even more shocked to read, in Levaux's account of their early acquaintance, Bloy's first letter to this young admirer of his, touching him for money before it has even transpired whether the young man has any. Levaux, charmingly, quotes the letter without appearing to think this odd and in fact, with his next letter, sent Bloy fifty francs.

This, however, is at least in character. Less easily forgiven – *pace* Maritain – is Bloy's lack of at any rate one kind of charity. The injunction to 'hate the sin and not the sinner' was ignored by him. Bloy hated the sinner and envisaged his eternal damnation with imperturbable self-satisfaction. Judging, Bloy lays himself open to judgment. He gloated. He gloated, for instance, over the fate he thought in store for the beautiful wives and daughters of the rich, to say nothing of the men to whom their favours were presumably accorded. The rich are hardly ever mentioned in this eschatological context without some image of a beautiful woman, deeply *décolletée* and sitting, perhaps, in her box at the Opéra. I have quoted Bloy's pleasure over the fire at the Opéra Comique. A similar pleasure was occasioned him by his morning paper on May the 5th, 1896, when he records:

Fire at the *Charity Bazaar*. A large number of fair ladies were carbonised, yesterday evening, in less than half an hour. *Non pro mundo rogo*, saith the Lord.

Four days later, he is still rejoicing, and he sends to André Rouveyre a lengthy document on the affair, in which he imagines all these '*chastes lys*' and '*tendres roses*' trampling each other in the attempt to get out. For a man of Bloy's powerful emotivity and instinct to dominate, the disadvantage he is at with desirable women may well be one of the chief drawbacks of a life of poverty, and an impulse of sadistic hatred (accompanied, so often, by images drawn from the privy) may be the inevitable response to privation so painful. But a sensitive and intelligent man could be expected to examine even his privations dispassionately at moments, and it is not Bloy's violence which repels so much as his persistence in it. If the rich are damned and the consolation of the poor certain, there is some reason to feel an occasional impulse of pity towards the rich and perhaps especially towards their womenfolk. A pity expended by a poor man exclusively upon the poor cannot be far removed from self-pity. There is in Bloy none of the tenderness we find in Blake, a man equally driven. His interest in individual poor people was slight. While he records once rescuing a dying man from the street, he betrays no curiosity about the lives of his neighbours and sets down nothing but the villainies of a succession of daily helps and caretakers.

The situation of Bloy's childhood was provided for him by a devout mother whom he loved, an anti-clerical father whom he did not love and loutish brothers who adopted the views of their father. Largely self-educated and without either money or polish, the young Bloy in Paris could only oppose to the gifts of others what they might accept as of a primitive force. He chose his faith. In the same way, D. H. Lawrence in London chose to personify the reputedly greater virility of the proletariat, especially miners. Bloy claimed that his was an improved faith, that what both laity and clergy offered lacked an ingredient known to him alone. Few accepted this claim. The general opinion was that the only difference between Bloy's faith and anybody else's was that Bloy's faith was more vociferously advertised. There remained only the proof of martyrdom. Bloy sought this in the only way normally open to a man of letters.

In the book of Simone Weil's to which reference has already been made, I read:

Another effect of affliction is, little by little, to make the soul its accomplice, by injecting a poison of inertia into it. In anyone who has suffered affliction for a long enough time there is a complicity with regard to his own affliction. . . Further, this complicity may even induce him to shun the means of deliverance. In such cases it veils itself with excuses which are often ridiculous. Even a person who has come through his affliction will still have something left in him which impels him to plunge into it again, if it has bitten deeply and for ever into the substance of his soul. . . If the affliction has been ended as a result of some kindness, it may take the form of hatred for the benefactor.

For the existence of this strange complicity, there are no doubt many of us who can personally vouch. Of the 'animal mechanism' involved, the curious history of Léon Bloy affords a great many examples.

The life he lived was a rigid, clenched life from which all that might tempt other people was banished. It narrowed Bloy's imagination, increasing the pressure in a few channels of obsession. We shall have to decide whether this was a pity or not. I think that, on the one hand, it produced a degree of blind dishonesty and, on the other, that it precluded any form of psychological development, spiritual growth or whatever our frames of reference may encourage us to call a gradual modification and refinement of our attitudes.

Take, for instance, the visions of Anne-Marie Roulet. Could the most firmly grounded enemy of psychologistic interpretations honestly find it unwarrantable to associate Anne-Marie's visions with her madness, at least in part, as symptom to malady? I take it that Bloy's mind established this link and that it was this perception which drove him to a greyer, emptier despair than any he has portrayed. For he was preparing to stake all on the prophecies of his mistress, when suddenly they were revealed as the obsessive phantasies of a madwoman. Later he returned to these visions without, apparently, thinking it necessary to break the link in his mind. He does not seem to have considered it worth his while to study what little was then known about the nature of mental disorders. To me, this demonstrates that he no longer cared whether the visions were true or false, from Heaven or from the heart of madness. Their content fitted in very well with the metaphysical scheme of things upon which he proposed to insist, and that was enough for him.

A price had to be paid. The Bloy affectionately described by Termier, Maritain, Levaux, is Bloy in old age, a little tamed but still claiming that the *literati* deliberately plot to starve him to death. Underneath, deeper impulses mined, those, for instance, which come to light in his writings on Napoleon. It is touching, too, to read how in later life Bloy was troubled with dreams of wealth – dreams in which he saw himself 'inundated with gold'. At the same time, if we put a high price on anything Bloy wrote, we cannot really deplore the narrowing which also resulted in a concentration. A life is a totality and every part of it equally necessary. At his best, Bloy was majestic. At his worst, there is something lovable about the old fraud.

If a publisher were to consult me on the best means of introducing the work of Léon Bloy to non-Catholic English readers, my advice would be that he should print first a slim volume of selected passages and then the journals sufficiently cut to bring them within the compass of two volumes. The great diarist of our time was André Gide. On the face of it, there is very little in common between Gide and Bloy. Delicate self-searching was not in Bloy's line. His was a highly emotive and not at all a subtle temperament. Compared with Gide, he was a simple soul. And yet it is, I think, true of both men that their journals most adequately represent them. Their other works seem like mere extensions to a vast autobiographical enterprise.

Gide's other works nevertheless make agreeable reading. Bloy's, on the whole, do not. He was perhaps too much what Raymond Mortimer would call 'an enemy of pleasure'. On the other hand, embedded in his works are certain passages of unparalleled splendour which are of the nature of poems. The idea of a prose-poem does not appeal to everybody – by and large, I would say rightly. The weakness of a prose-poem is generally its looseness of form. The poems of Léon Bloy, though in prose, are not loose. They are, for a start, bound together by their diction, which is as highly wrought and incidentally as Latinate as Milton's.

The two-volume journals would exhibit Bloy in all his cantankerousness and discomfort. They would show what Maritain meant by describing his godfather as a Christian of the second century strayed into the Third Republic. They would also provide a valuable check on the literary history of the period, whose tones are muted by the textbooks. Bloy's hatred was excessive. But so was the veneration accorded to Parisian men of letters in the late nineteenth century. The exasperation of Bloy is frequently illuminating. There is also something not to be found elsewhere in the sense which Bloy gives us of a fanatically constant personality. In Gide, what fascinates is change, evasion, dispersal and re-integration. In Bloy, it is the play of changing circumstances upon a man of few attitudes, rigid and defiant.

Of the passages clamouring for inclusion in a small volume, I have already mentioned the crucifixion in *Le Salut par les Juifs* and the epithalamion in *La Femme Pauvre*. From the introduction to *La Vie de Mélanie*, the great letter to his fiancée of November the 27th, 1889, and the passage on the animals in *La Femme Pauvre*, I have quoted. From *L'Ame de Napoléon*, we should have to take a tremendous eve-of-battle scene, in which the French army sleeping upon the plains of Poland is seen as 'an immense herd of souls, beasts of the field of Eternity'; later, they die in battle, thronging about Napoleon, 'who brushes them away with his hand like importunate thoughts'. From *Le Désespéré*, we should take the revelation, '*durant l'oisive chaufferie de pieds d'une nuit de grand-garde en 1870*', of the momentary powerlessness of God. From the same work, there would be a description of the Grande Chartreuse. From *La Femme Pauvre*, in addition to the epithalamion and the animals, there would be a scene at mass in which the priest going sleepily through his routine appears to speak to Clotilde as a representative of the sleeping church.

Larger volumes of selected passages from Bloy have appeared in French. Béguin published one in Switzerland during the war. Recently, Raïssa Maritain put out a copious *Pages de Léon Bloy*, with an introduction by Jacques Maritain which is in fact his old piece served up again. To my taste, both volumes too fully represent Bloy as a theologian and as a critical thinker. In the Maritain compilation, *L'Exégèse des Lieux Communs* is, I would say, over-prominent. Yet even our small volume would have to include one or two of these pieces. It would also have to include one of the *Histoires Désobligeantes*. Anti-*bourgeois* stories in a similar vein and for the most part not true stories, these yet seem to prefigure the Jouhandeau of *Les Pincengrains*. Even the books which are largely devoted to invective against the writers of the time contain anthology pieces. From *Les Dernières Colonnes de l'Eglise*, we should take a description of the beggar's entry into Heaven, from *Belluaires et Porchers* a passage on Verlaine's poetry and from *La Résurrection de Villiers de l'Isle-Adam* an account of the fair promise of Villiers' early days (apart from Hello, Villiers de l'Isle-Adam and Verlaine were the only two of his literary contemporaries whom Bloy always cherished). *Le Sang du Pauvre* would need to be represented more fully than any other work, for here the vision is sustained.

The creative process operated strangely in Bloy. Deficient in any ordinary sense of construction, he wrote slowly, never revising. Apart from the two novels, those of his books which are not mere collections of articles and sketches are short. In the early, very brief chapters, he jerkily intoxicates and hypnotises himself and is presently embarked upon the poem which thereafter dominates his book, so that the more tentative exordium and peroration could sometimes be detached without loss. Or perhaps it is not so much intoxication as disintoxication. For the opening and closing chapters are those in which Bloy thrusts his opinions at us. Opinions are intellectual chains. Bloy's opinions were singularly heavy. The creative process is always at war with opinion. Bloy's creative rhythm is nowhere so perfectly apparent as in *Le Salut par les Juifs*, but it is everywhere present. For so opinionated a man as Bloy, it was necessary. It is the organic rhythm of trance, of athletic feats, of anaesthesia, of mystical experience, of itch and orgasm, of delirium and the epileptic fit.

In *La Femme Pauvre*, Bloy describes his own style in that of Marchenoir and speaks of:

43

La violente couleur de l'écrivain, sa barbarie cauteleuse et alam-
biquée; l'insistance giratoire, l'enroulement têtu de certaines images
cruelles revenant avec obstination sur elles-mêmes comme les convolvu-
lacées; l'audace inouïe de cette forme, nombreuse autant qu'une horde
et si rapide, quoique pesamment armée; le tumulte sage de ce vocabu-
laire panaché de flammes et de cendres ainsi que le Vésuve aux derniers
jours de Pompéi, balafré d'or, incrusté, denticulé de gemmes antiques,
a la façon d'une châsse de martyr; mais surtout l'élargissement prodi-
gieux qu'un pareil style conférait soudain à la moins ambitieuse des
thèses, au postulat le plus infime et le plus acclimaté.

I shall refrain from attempting a translation of this passage.
Its exuberance is un-French, and yet it belongs so perfectly to
this language of epithet that English could hardly deal with it.
Bloy started life as a painter and engraver. He implies several
times that this accounts for his way of writing. In this I think
he is wrong, unless we are to see him laying on words like ena-
mel. Inscribing a book for one of his admirers, he wrote that he
was 'a poet and nothing but a poet'. At other times, he indignantly rejects the notion that he is an artist at all. He is simply,
he says, 'a pilgrim of the Holy Sepulchre', and he denies all
possibility of a 'Christian art', which, he says, if it were conceiv-
able, would be nothing less than 'a gate open on Paradise'.
Music, on the other hand, which is not the music of religious
devotion is either revolting or meaningless. He dreamed, nevertheless, of literary glory. He expected to be read with enthusiasm
in two or three hundred years – odd, you might think, for a
man hourly expecting the world to come to an end. And in
this mood he says:

Art is all that remains. An art, it is true, despised and kept
down, starved, fugitive and in rags, an art of the catacombs.
All the same, it is the sole refuge of a few exceptionally lofty
souls doomed to drag their sick carcases over the carrion-
strewn crossroads of the world.

The incantatory use of Latin in Bloy's prose is not unrelated
to the liturgical drone which is heard like a beat-note in the

44

canticles of Paul Claudel and, in English, of T. S. Eliot. Bloy's French is conspicuous for its inversions and perhaps especially for his thrusting of the adjective before the noun, a trick, radically alien to the language, which French writers have increasingly used for special emphasis, but none, so far as I can recall, as frequently and as defiantly as Bloy. On these stylistic points, however, I am content to leave the last word to the French themselves.

The importance of Bloy in the tradition of French literature may be more hopefully estimated by a foreigner. This is not purely a question of contemporary or posthumous influence. A writer may be important not so much for what he has done as for what other writers have left undone. And this may be through no merit of his own. It may be a matter of historical or topographical accident. Unique, Bloy certainly was. In modern times, no Frenchman has written prose so riotously excessive. At no time since the Dark Ages has any Catholic written with such apocalyptical fixity of vision. At no time has anybody more rigorously defied his age and yet not ended in mere bitterness and defeat. We cannot deny Bloy the interest due to a freak, an eccentric, a Caliban of letters. At least

> We'll have thee as our rarer monsters are,
> Painted upon a pole and underwrit:
> 'Here ye may see — '

There was, it is true, around Bloy, at the time of his literary beginnings, a climate of Catholic romanticism. He was conspicuously influenced by Barbey d'Aurevilly, to whom he admitted to owing what he calls his return to the faith, but which we may be tempted to describe as a perception that it was possible to put the trappings of faith to a literary purpose. In a recent issue of *La Table Ronde*, a critic, reviewing Bollery's third hagiographical study, finds that the name of Bloy now conjures up 'a whole literary epoch, that of the Christian-symbolist amalgam, anarchy, neurosis and an oratorical humour'. Bloy's distinction was to shed the obvious mystification, diabolism and ecclesiastical foppery of his master and to show that

45

a gesture and a pose might also be devised for an emphatic literalness of belief. This has carried forward. French literary Catholicism now is of the most *croyant*. Nothing could be more earnest than the half-predestinating Jansenism of Mauriac or Bernanos' wrestling with visible devils. The poets, from Claudel to Pierre Emmanuel, have perhaps indulged myths of their own, but even the self-consciously bad Catholics like Jouhandeau, although it is not isolation through poverty they practice, yet practise an isolation they may have learnt from Bloy. Gabriel Marcel flirts with the existentialist approach, but somehow never fails to reach the orthodox conclusion. Bloy wrote bad novels, but he started the Catholic novel. Claudel applied his metaphysical symbolism to the drama and later turned to exegesis of the kind which Bloy had practised. Graham Greene's most recent novel, *The End of the Affair*, bears an epigraph from Bloy:

Man has places in his heart which do not yet exist, and into them enters suffering in order that they may have existence.

We may suppose that Mr Greene feels that this statement in some way embodies the essence of what he himself is trying to convey.

That Bloy had a message for at any rate some of his co-religionists is therefore certain. This message was not at once assimilated. Bloy, in his time, was a great worry to the Catholic party in France. A little over a week ago, I purchased from the holy literature stall in the small and charming cathedral of St Jean-de-Maurienne a book published just after the war by a firm shamelessly calling itself '*la bonne presse*' and concerned to urge the claims of La Salette. In this book Bloy, who so rigorously championed these claims, goes unmentioned. Such neglect is, however, vestigial. Since Bloy's death, a double change has taken place. Catholic intellectuals are now more serious. They have adopted the absoluteness of Bloy. On the other hand, they have also become more orthodox. Every effort has therefore been made to remove from Bloy the breath of scandal. The monster has been rendered innocuous. Catholic critics have explained what he really meant and that his angrier or more heterodox utterances were a rhetoric designed to press home the eternal verities. In Catholic literary circles, to approve of Bloy is now itself a *bondieuserie*. His very tone of voice is imitated by those who have earned no right to it by any intransigence of life.

Where there is no question of literary influence, the nature of Bloy's message to his co-religionists is a little obscure. Béguin dedicates his book on Bloy to Stanislas Fumet (who also wrote one) 'in fellowship of impatience'. This I take to mean that M. Béguin is, and understands M. Fumet to be, revolted by the world in which he lives and impatient for apocalyptical change of the kind predicted by Bloy. Elsewhere, one has the impression that Bloy is being fêted as a champion. There are situations in which every Englishman feels that he wrote the plays of Shakespeare, every Scotsman that he won the battle of Bannockburn. Every Anglican intellectual is now a Kierkegaard, every Catholic book-reviewer a Léon Bloy. It is a misappropriation not so much of literary property as of *mana*. It is some kind of prowess in which Bloy is felt to have excelled. He was a champion believer. He believed harder and more continuously than his co-religionists could. He discharges their incapacity.

What he believed is probably safe enough. On all major points of doctrine, Bloy affirms his submission to the Holy Office, though he did not, as Catholic publicists now do, seek an official *nihil obstat* and *imprimatur*. There is a tendency to Manichaeism in his distaste for a very large part of the created world and in his presentation of the rich as incurably evil, but of a ripe and explicit heresy it would probably not be possible to convict him. In his life-time, he was accused of conforming to the heresy of Vintras, who had postulated a coming incarnation of the Holy Ghost, but Bloy indignantly repudiated this. About the apparition at La Salette he was reckless, but in a foreword to *Celle Qui Pleure* he writes:

In my capacity as a Catholic, I hereby declare that I submit entirely to the teaching of the Church, to the rulings and

47

decisions of the Holy See, notably the decretals of the Sovereign Pontiffs Urban VIII and Benedict XIV concerning the canonisation of Saints.

Elsewhere there are traces of a suspicious philosophical idealism, but they are not grave.

That a Catholic writer may appear to non-Catholic readers to have a message for themselves is currently demonstrated by the success of Graham Greene. It is not merely that Mr Greene, a successful novelist, also happens to be a Catholic (like Evelyn Waugh, who for the most part has kept his Catholicism and his novel-writing apart). It is precisely the two recent books of his, in which his Catholicism is most stressed, which have gained Mr Greene the widest admiration. Before that, despite his latent popularity through films, he remained something of a highbrow figure. Perhaps if we analysed this situation, we should be able to gauge the likelihood of a writer like Bloy seeming to have something to communicate to the British reading public.

First, we must, I think, be clear in our minds that the common reader in England is not altogether and perhaps not at all representative of non-Catholic readers elsewhere. In France, for instance, we like to think that there exists such a thing as informed anti-clerical opinion. At any rate, most Frenchmen have had the opportunity of discovering what the doctrines and practices of Catholicism are. In England, it is otherwise. It is not a question of the differences between Catholic and Protestant belief. It is rather that any literalness or distinctness of belief has, for centuries, been socially discouraged among us. If a member of the Church of England or, for that matter, of one of the reformed churches upheld the specific teachings of his church in the same way as a Catholic, he and the Catholic would enjoy a basis for mutual understanding (and perhaps for mutual hatred) at present denied them by the fact that hardly any Englishman considers it necessary to know what he believes. Religion is, to him, at best a feeling of metaphysical cosiness accompanied by a desire to be unselfish. If pressed, he will usually yield the opinion that Our Lord was a quite exceptionally good man and that it would be an excellent thing for all of us if we behaved rather more as he is said to have wished us to. The idea of, for instance, immortality is associated in his mind with youth and first love and does not thereafter persist except in maiden aunts and persons unbalanced by grief.

If an Englishman, as a result of foreign travel or of his sister marrying an Irishman, catches a glimpse of Catholics at their devotions, he is generally repelled by the pictures and the candles and worried by the confessional, which appears to him a furtive and unwholesome device of priestly ambition. The Catholics are, he supposes, Christians like himself, but questions of doctrine not only do not present themselves to his mind but would seem to him not at all to the point, unless it were, perhaps, the clearly nonsensical and mischievous doctrine that the Pope is infallible. He may also have gathered that at holy communion Catholics think that the insipid bread and thin wine not merely symbolise but actually turn into the body and blood of Our Lord.

Across a gulf as wide as this, it hardly seems possible that intercourse of any kind should take place. Here, English good manners come in. I do not mean that English manners are exceptionally good, but simply that English good manners were devised for coping with precisely this kind of awkwardness. English tolerance is tolerance of belief. It is not tolerance of behaviour. In matters of behaviour, the English have long been noted for their intolerance. But they do not question other people's beliefs. They do not think well of the way Catholics behave in their churches, but their doctrinal reasons for so behaving are quite safe from English scrutiny. Since 1864, this has been true even among intellectuals. A clergyman by the name of Kingsley thought, as he well might, that, if a man as well educated and intelligent as the Reverend J. H. Newman professed adherence to these foreign superstitions, it could only be out of affectation. A full-sized controversy took place, and Newman incontestably won on points. The result of Kingsley's discomfiture has been that, to the Englishman's natural or acquired disinclination to enquire into other people's beliefs, there is added, among intellectuals, a conviction that the nature

49

of belief is itself complicated and that only Catholics properly understand it.

Catholic writers nevertheless thrive in England, and Graham Greene has been only the more successful the more his work has incorporated what is understood to be a theological element. Are we therefore to suppose that the English common reader is now avid for Catholic doctrine, so long as it is served up to him in a popular form which relates it to the lives of individual men and women? I do not think so. The popularity of religious novelists in the past has never meant that faith was on the increase. Hall Caine and R. H. Benson were dying echoes of the Oxford movement. Yet to-day's common reader must be avid for something which Mr Greene is able to supply and which he supplies in part by virtue of the fact that he is a Catholic.

His Catholicism apart, what are Mr Greene's characteristics as a novelist? He divides his own work into two kinds. His more serious books he allows to be described as novels. His lighter books he calls 'entertainments'. These entertainments are generally about gangsters or spies, and a number of them have been turned into first-rate gangster or spy films. But even in Mr Greene's 'novels' crime or the psychological accompaniment of crime also predominates. In *The Power and the Glory*, the drunken priest is no less on the run than the hare-lipped killer of *A Gun for Sale*. Mr Greene's first novel was about a man on the run at the beginning of the nineteenth century. In *Brighton Rock*, which is classified as a novel, the young gangster hero is contrasted favourably with even the most agreeable of the virtuous characters on the ground that, since he is a Catholic, he can be damned. Even in *The Heart of the Matter*, circumstances so close around Scobie that he feels himself to be hounded. A private detective is the most engaging figure in *The End of the Affair*, and it is to escape from the persecution of her lover that Sarah perambulates widely in the rain and so catches her death of pneumonia. Fear, anxiety and pursuit, the monotonous accompaniment of so many dreams, equally dominate the writings of Graham Greene.

With his earlier novels and entertainments, Mr Greene pleased at two levels, the lowest (that of the film-scenarist) and the *avant-garde*. With his later work, he has captured the larger middle public. This is a public whose reading matter must first of all be respectable. It does not permit itself pornography or any other kind of unpleasantness. Or rather, it does not permit itself what it recognises as pornography and unpleasantness. On the other hand, critics have detected a concealed pornographic (sadistical) element in the writings of such earlier favourites of this public as Ethel M. Dell. To many English people, there is a sub-erotic element in Catholicism itself, if only because they do not know what really goes on and are therefore able to fear the worst. The darkness of Catholic churches, the deeper shades of the confessional, are suggestive. The alleged misbehaviour of priests, monks and nuns has figured largely in the literature of Catholic countries themselves from Chaucer and Boccaccio to Balzac and Liam O'Flaherty. These elements do not loom in Mr Greene's work. If they did, the great British public of to-day would not read him. They read him because he tells them of prodigious dramas of conscience in Wimbledon and colonial Africa.

I feel sure that Mr Greene's purpose is serious. He is a wonderfully accomplished story-teller. He might not be so widely read if he wrote less well, and it is the evident profundity of the problems with which his characters are to be seen grappling which appeals to his new public. But the reaction of this public to Mr Greene's presentation of these problems must be extremely vague. We may, I think, take it that reviewers in the literary weeklies and the solider Sunday newspapers understand what they read a little better than most of the people for whom they write. Yet, when a translation from Mauriac or a novel by Mr Greene appears, they always trot out one phrase which is evidently felt to cover all such cases of profundity in the novel (they formerly used it for Charles Williams). Mr Greene's subject, they say (or M. Mauriac's subject), is 'the conflict between good and evil'. Whether Mr Greene's (or M. Mauriac's) view of what is good and what is evil corresponds in any respect with their own is a question our critics would find pedantic, and so would their readers. Both experience, at one and the same time, a sense of moral worth and a delicious glimpse of inaccessible and possibly forbidden depths. Mr Greene writes two kinds of shockers, those with guns and those with holy emotion. In both, we shudder with vicarious fright, here of the killer in the night, there of sin and damnation. The use to which this superb technician puts his religious faith meets with our full approval. Into the precise content of that faith, we do not enquire.

If we did, we might be disappointed. Mr Greene may believe that he personally will go to Hell if he commits adultery and subsequently goes to communion without confessing his fault and duly receiving absolution for it. His publication of such a novel as *The Heart of the Matter* does not, however, commit him to this belief. It commits him merely to supposing it credible that a colonial administrator, who is a Catholic, should subscribe to this belief and feel anxiety in this situation. Of course, Mr Greene seems to be recommending the belief to us. He thinks, we feel, that people ought to believe this, painful as it may occasionally be to do so. But does he really believe it himself? We shall never know. Through his skill in the presentation of imaginary situations, we have passed vicariously through an emotional crisis of a kind which does not arise in our own lives. We may even feel inferior because we do not take such things with quite the same agonising seriousness. Only a masochist on the clinical scale, however, would in real life torment himself in this way without having first innocently subscribed to the technical point of doctrine on which the situation is based, namely, whether it is mortal to participate in the sacraments without truthful confession and true repentance.

In his latest novel, *The End of the Affair*, Mr Greene ventures upon the question of belief itself. On behalf of his principal woman character, he states the problem in a curious passage, one sentence of which (the last here quoted) has greatly appealed to the reviewers.

> I believe the whole bag of tricks, there's nothing I don't believe, they could subdivide the Trinity into a dozen parts and I'd believe. They could dig up records that proved Christ had been invented by Pilate to get himself promoted and I'd believe just the same. I've caught belief like a disease.

52

But *what* would Sarah then believe? She would surely not believe that there existed one God in thirty-six persons or that a figment basely conceived in the mind of Pontius Pilate was at the same time the only son of this God, being also God in his own right or at least persons thirteen to twenty-four of God inclusive, persons twenty-five to thirty-six having been responsible for putting the idea into Pilate's head. Does she therefore believe, now, that there exists one God in three persons and that the second of these persons was parthenogenetically born as a male child a little under two thousand years ago? Or is it simply that she believes something else and that she is therefore prepared, in all further questions, to follow a party line laid down by those whom she finds least sceptical of what she believes, namely, that her prayer restored Bendrix to life? Only Mr Greene could tell us, for Sarah and her belief were invented by him, not, we may suppose, for the sake of promotion, of which he stands in no need.

It is, at any rate, in a Catholicism ambiguously propounded that the English common reader's interest at present lies. The same interest would hardly lead him to Léon Bloy, for whom the verb 'to believe' was unquestionably transitive. To the non-Catholic reader disinclined to approach Catholicism more directly, Bloy must, I fancy, remain a closed book. There are, however, three other main varieties of non-Catholic reader. There is the enquiring and perhaps bewildered reader, the potential convert, who would like to examine the Catholic religion carefully but from a position of safety. There is (perhaps) the informed and convinced anti-clerical, who would nevertheless like to have a working basis for his relations with Catholics. And there is the person who, devoted to another spiritual discipline, perhaps within the Protestant communion or perhaps attached by tradition or personal inclination to one of the oriental religions, yet safely welcomes whatever he finds positive and attractive in the Roman rite. The numbers of non-Catholics of this kind are likely to be increased by the influence of Simone Weil, who has shown (in my opinion, with far greater validity than the agents of Anglo-Catholic *rapprochement*, upon whom still lies the mantle of pre-Raphaelite ecclesiastical foppery) just how close

53

one may come without abandonment to the official theology and, moreover, without recourse to the official channels of grace.

To the enquirer, what is most personal in this essay may serve as a warning. Explicitly, I would say that, while he expresses possibilities always latent in Catholicism, Bloy is nevertheless unrepresentative and perhaps dangerously so, not only by his positive excesses but by his omissions. What he omits is not only the more unattractive side of Catholicism. He omits almost the whole of Christian morality. This suggests that there may have been a curious Lutheran side to his religious temperament – odd in a man who inveighed so terribly against the 'Lutheran hordes' of Germany. He would never have preached justification through faith, but he often seems to exemplify it. With this goes his Manichaean tendency. The history of Manichaeism in Christendom is a strange one. The zealots who arise preaching the incurably evil nature of the created world generally do so from the purest motives. Their followers, however, tend to reason that, if the physical world is of its nature evil, it matters not at all what we do with the body. Luther's teaching that man in his fallen state can achieve no good by himself but must be compelled by divine grace leans heavily to the Manichaean side. Faith is all. The attempted performance of works is futile. Where a secular morality of no particular theological inspiration prevails, the orgiastic tendencies inherent in this doctrine, the revelling in self-abasement, confident of justification by faith, are held in check. In chaotic societies and among the underprivileged, they may lead not merely to the lack of a sufficient morality but to fanatical immorality. Franz Borkenau has shown how the hold of Rasputin on the last Russian court drew its strength from theology of this kind.

Bloy came out of the aesthetic period in French Catholicism. He was in part an iconoclast. His morality consisted in being 'absolute'. It tended to situate him on the justification-through-faith side of *ama et fac quod vis*, which is a safe enough doctrine if we insist sufficiently upon the nature of love and which, even if we do not, remains better than *crede et fac quod vis*. Lutheran doctrine produces and is metaphysical schizophrenia. The Catholic church wisely insists on the goodness or at any rate the

54

moral indifference of the physical world and requires human co-operation in grace. Bloy, who made converts, might therefore turn away potential converts of a different temperament. To me, this has in itself become a matter of indifference, but an attachment to mere truth should prevent us from wishing people to be turned away from any object of their study by an unfortunate choice of reading matter.

Those whose minds are made up against the church may do better with Bloy. There is in his insistence on poverty as the only virtuous state and in his metaphysic of money something which finds its echo in a great many of·the most resolutely agnostic and indeed materialistic minds. Most denunciations of the rich sound false. It is not merely that we suspect the denouncers of wishing to be rich. It is also that the arguments they use to show what evils are brought about by accumulations of power and wealth are merely empirical. It is easy to counter them with demonstrations both of what practical good has been effected by concentrated wealth and of how little difference a redistribution of wealth could be expected to make. That poverty is essentially a holy condition and that riches constitute an insuperable barrier to salvation are ideas which the church has never openly denounced. A cult of poverty underlay the monastic orders at their foundation. The desert fathers knew it, and its desirability is borne in upon Protestants by their study of the Bible. For poverty was clearly enjoined by the Jesus whom all Christian sects regard as, in one sense or another, the founder of their religion. The texts are numerous, and toleration of the rich has been one of the most persistent of those scandals which have led to schism and apostasy throughout the Christian era. Alas, schismatics and apostates change their tune as soon as they have become successful. In the end, they join with the church in a tacit conspiracy to shelve this awkward issue. They deal empirically and take every advantage of the weakness of empiricism. Bloy's vision of a cannibalistic universe, whose diabolical eucharist is the blood of the poor beneath the species of money, is not only grandiose; it is also, so far as I can see, incontrovertible.

Our time has seen it curiously blurred. In England at least, there has been a largely successful attempt to abolish the extremes of poverty. The poor are no longer with us in quite the sense in which they are with Ireland, Spain and even France. The complaints of some who were formerly rich has also given rise to the opinion that nobody is rich any longer. This paragraph is written on British polling day, October 25th, 1951. What changes in the social and political scene may have taken place before the whole essay is published, I cannot tell. Last night, however, I walked through the west end of London with two people from the country who had not visited the time-kept city for over a year. We were agreed that within that time there had appeared a larger number than even before the war of obvious and disgusting rich. The operations of the vampire may have been obscured. It may be that a larger number of people have felt the vile lips upon them and yet that nobody is for the moment sucked completely dry. It may be, too, that we have learnt new ways of being rich and poor. We are all apocalyptically minded now, having discovered that we live in the atomic age. So far the discovery seems only to have increased our self-pity and diminished our compassion, so that we devise ways unknown to Bloy whereby one man can plunge another into affliction, even if their bank balances are identical. The same or with a difference, the hideous feast goes on.

This aspect of Bloy's vision is valid for everybody. His embodiment of it in his exegesis of the *clichés* by which for the most part we live is always suggestive, even when, for ourselves, we might be led to a different reading. About a specific relation of Bloy to spiritual disciplines outside Catholicism, I write tentatively and with extreme diffidence. I had better make it clear that I write under influence, under an influence which I am bound to recognise may be wholly temporary for me. This is the influence of Simone Weil, whose work I have been reading with a good deal of attention since I first quoted her. Reviewing the first English translation of Simone Weil in the *New Statesman and Nation*, Graham Greene dismisses this extraordinary young woman as a muddle-headed prig. I feel that, in doing this, Mr Greene is following an imaginary party line. The French Catholics have treated Simone Weil with an exemplary liberality of mind. Her works have been issued largely under Catholic auspices and are to be seen displayed in the *bondieuserie* shops in the Rue St Sulpice. This *Attente de Dieu*, now translated into English, nevertheless consists in the main of the young philosophy teacher's reasons for not joining the church. It is a curious position. Sooner or later, one feels, the Vatican will be driven either to beatify a non-Catholic or to put her writings on the Index. Mr Greene anticipates.

For the moment, Simone Weil convinces me, as I have not been convinced for some fourteen years, that to speak of one's 'spiritual life' is not merely and inevitably to make a priggish and disagreeable noise. On the face of it, she and Bloy stand in marked opposition to each other. I cannot imagine what Bloy would have made of Simone Weil, though he treated another intelligent young Jewess, Raïssa Maritain, sensitively and with positive effect. Simone Weil appears to have left no written comment on Bloy. She would certainly have found him excessively given to idolatry of the church as an institution. The Providence which Bloy attempted to see in every line of history was for Simone Weil merely a form of '*l'imagination combleuse de vides*'. To Simone Weil, personality was opaque and therefore evil. To Bloy, sainthood itself was but individuality carried to its extreme limit. The language of Simone Weil was rigorously simplified and denuded. Bloy not only practised but also preached exaggeration.

> The evil of this world is not properly seen unless we exaggerate it. . . An artist who views only the object itself *does not see it*. . . Hyperbole is a microscope for scrutinising insects and a telescope for bringing us near the stars.

Of Simone Weil's utter sincerity, I am convinced. Of Bloy's, I am frequently doubtful. There may well be temperaments to which all this gorgeousness and reiteration will seem transparent. Through it, to them, the light of another world may appear to shine. To most of us in Britain, it is, I fancy, more likely to suggest new varieties of idolatrous affirmation. We are a people already prone to such affirmations, especially north of the

57

Tweed, west of the Severn and in the higher income groups. If we gave him a chance, Bloy could nevertheless teach us a good deal about 'the assertion of what we know to be untrue for purposes of emotional satisfaction'. The difference would be that Bloy related all he desired and the whole of his *imagination combleuse* to a system of ideas which had been true for millions of people over a period of nineteen hundred years, a system which the drip of time has somewhat purified.

For any foreign spiritual discipline, Bloy would have entertained no regard. For the Greeks, both ancient and modern, he displayed nothing but contempt, while Simone Weil found their imagination from the beginning full of 'pre-Christian intuitions'. The Russians Bloy considered abominable schismatics, the only possible justification for whose existence was that they might have damaged England if they had not mistaken their historical mission and attacked Japan. We can only imagine his reaction to the suggestion that Indian, Chinese or Islamic mysticism had anything to teach us, though even in this connection we may find in the journals one passage which apparently contradicts the rest. After seeing a Javanese exhibition, Bloy says that it reminded him of certain works of Indian art and that all these products convince him that their originators have only just left the Garden of Eden. Bloy is like this. It is hardly possible to imagine a contradiction not somewhere discernible in his work. As to Kierkegaard and the Anglican community, he would allow no good thing to have come out of Denmark except his wife or out of England except soldiers. Faced even with English Catholicism (in the novels of R. H. Benson), he at first admires but in the end can only find it 'septentrional, Cimmerian, hyperborean', and withdraw into his own Latinity. The Jews he accommodated only after conversion. *Anathema sit* was often on his lips. He perpetually instances Simone Weil's principal objection to the Catholic church, that it is precisely not catholic. It seems likely that, to those trained in a foreign discipline, the only lesson he could teach would be that of exclusiveness.

In the end, it will be for pagan reasons that we admire Bloy if we admire him at all. It will be for his charm as a monster, his force as a prototype. The world has grown slippery. To affirm constantly and in the absolute anything but a local super-stition is unknown to-day amongst men of letters. In our time, D. H. Lawrence tried to do it, but lacked the physique. George Orwell tried with less conviction still and died of the same disease, which is essentially a disease of discouragement. To such men, we are forced to listen. The longer they vociferate, the more valuable they are, whatever it is they may be trying to communicate and however full of contradiction we find them. They begin to exercise a siren power upon us deaf and sinuous adders. We stiffen. We lift our heads. We may even try to stand upright in the position recommended to human beings. This is the great virtue of the boring and the provincial in literature. We are reduced to nonentity by the interesting and the metropolitan.

The uses of a prototype may be equally positive or negative and are sometimes both. Léon Bloy bequeathed us a pattern of life in some respects forever valid. He was in other respects what we perhaps insensitively call 'a horrid warning'. He wagered heavily and broke somewhat less than even. We shall not imitate him exactly. We may hope to profit from his losses. As Middleton Murry would say, 'he lived through his experience for us'. As for me, now that I have brought this essay to its close, I shall hope to dispose of Bloy in red buckram too, though he may still turn out to be *l'Invendable*. I doubt whether, in any case, it will mean that I have finished with him for good. Upon those exposed at a tender age to so powerful an irritant, it may well be that the delayed effects are incurable.

BIOGRAPHICAL NOTE

1846 Birth of Léon Bloy on the 12th July at Périgueux.
Apparition of the Blessed Virgin Mary at La Salette on the 19th September.

1863 In Paris.

1867 Death of Baudelaire on the 31st August.

1869 Meeting with Barbey d'Aurevilly, and 'conversion'.

1870 In the army of the Loire.

1871-1873 At Périgueux.

1877 Employed in the Société des Chemins de Fer du Nord, first meetings with Anne-Marie Roulet and the Abbé Tardif de Moidrey, retreat at La Trappe.

1878 Further retreat at La Trappe.

1879 First visit to La Salette, death of the Abbé Tardif de Moidrey.

1882 Anne-Marie incarcerated on the 1st July.

1883-1885 Regular contributions to *Le Chat Noir*, liaison with, and death from lock-jaw of Berthe Dumont.

1887 Opéra Comique gutted by fire on the 25th May. *Le Désespéré.*

1889 Deaths of Villiers de l'Isle-Adam and Barbey d'Aurevilly, first meeting with Jeanne Molbech.

1890 Marriage to Jeanne Molbech on the 11th June.

1891 First visit to Denmark.

1892 *Le Salut par les Juifs.*

1896 Death of Verlaine on the 8th January, death of son Pierre on the 24th September.

1897 *La Femme Pauvre.*

1899-1900 Second visit to Denmark.

1900-1904 At Lagny-sur-Marne.

1902 *L'Exégèse des Lieux Communs*, death of Emile Zola on the 29th September.

1904 Death of Mélanie Calvat on the 14th December.

1906 At La Salette from the 10th to the 25th August.

1907 Death of Anne-Marie Roulet on the 7th May, death of J. K. Huysmans on the 12th May.

1908 *Celle Qui Pleure.*

1909 *Le Sang du Pauvre.*

1910 At La Salette from the 15th to the 17th June.

1911 At St Expédit, revisits Périgueux.

1912 *L'Ame de Napoléon, La Vie de Mélanie.*

1913 *L'Exégèse des Lieux Communs* (Second Series).

1917 Death, at Bourg-la-Reine, on the 3rd November.

BIBLIOGRAPHICAL NOTE

Apart from his journals, the most important works of Léon Bloy are listed above with the dates of their publication. Most of the books about him are referred to in the text. The best of them is probably Fumet's. There is an English translation of Béguin. The non-Catholic reader who has recourse to any of the Catholic accounts of Bloy would, however, do well to balance its effect by also reading Seillière. Léon Bloy's total output was large. Rather little of it is to be found in print at any given moment, and that little is not always representative. The Maritain *Pages de Léon Bloy* is likely to prove better introductory value than anything turned up by casual enquiry at even the larger bookshops in Paris.